ARMY HOSPITAL SHIPS

Monograph prepared by
Mr. Harold Larson
Office of the Chief of Transportation
Army Service Forces
December 1944

Published by Books Express Publishing
Copyright © Books Express, 2011
ISBN 978-1-78039-500-5

Books Express publications are available from all good retail and online booksellers. For
publishing proposals and direct ordering please contact us at: info@books-express.com

This monograph was prepared prior to October 1946 from documentary material then available. It is not to be considered a final report, therefore, nor has it been thoroughly edited. Reproduction has been authorized in order that the information may be made available to military schools pending the publication of the official history of the Transportation Corps.

Persons finding in this manuscript errors of fact or important omissions are requested to communicate with the Historical Branch, Office of the Chief of Transportation and submit information which will be helpful in making appropriate corrections.

CONTENTS

PHOTOGRAPHS

FOREWORD

This monograph is based almost entirely upon the files of the War Department, supplemented in some instances by information obtained orally from certain individuals with special knowledge of the Army hospital ships. In particular, considerable assistance was derived from the staff and records of the Water Division, Office of the Chief of Transportation, Army Service Forces. In addition, the Medical Regulating Officer, Office of the Surgeon General, Army Service Forces, placed his inactive files at the disposal of the writer.

At present, five additional vessels have been selected for conversion into Army hospital ships. The conversion program, as extended, will not be accomplished until the spring or early summer of 1945, but represents no radical departure from the procedure already developed. Accordingly, it has appeared advisable to close the account at this point, since further developments may be incorporated in an addendum of a later date.

HAROLD LARSON

The Pentagon
December 1944

HISTORICAL BACKGROUND

The evacuation of the sick and wounded is a perennial problem in the history of warfare. The initial phase of such evacuation, namely, the assembling of patients from the battlefield, has long been and still is the task of the litter bearers. To carry on beyond the preliminary phase of collecting the sick and the wounded, the United States Army, in common with other armies, has resorted to various forms of transport ranging from animal and motor-drawn ambulances to hospital trains, vessels, and airplanes—all designed to bring the patients to a place where they can receive adequate medical attention.[1]

The purpose of this brief account is to describe the complex process of evacuation solely as it involves water transportation, and, more particularly, the use during the current conflict of Army hospital ships enjoying a protected status under international agreements. Important though their role is, it should be understood at the outset that Army hospital ships return to the United States only a small portion of the sick and wounded of the armed forces. Practically every returning Army transport carries patients;[2] and the Air Transport Command, Army Air

---

[1] On the transportation of patients in time of war, see Edgar E. Hume, Victories of Army Medicine (Philadelphia, 1943), pp. 148-150.

[2] Beginning early in 1944, in order to provide overseas commanders with usable data for evacuating patients by sea, the Water Division, OCT, at Washington D. C. (Maintenance and Repair Branch), at the instance of the Movements Division, OCT, and in conjunction with the ports of embarkation, has had compiled the patient capacity inbound of each personnel transport (carrying 50 passengers or more) in the service of the Army (OCT Form No. 46, 21 January 1944). See TC Circular 80-12, 22 January 1944 and Misc. Letter No. 28, OCT, 14 July 1944.

Forces, brings back the sick and wounded regularly by airplane. More-over, in addition to its own fleet of convention-protected hospital ships, the Navy utilizes hospital spaces on its own transports for the evacuation of patients by water. For evacuation by air the Navy relies upon the Naval Air Transportation Service.

The Civil War

The first extensive use of vessels by the United States Army for the transportation of sick and wounded personnel dates from the Civil War. The large number of casualties necessitated considerable hospitali-zation at points along the coast and near the inland waterways, and early in the war hospital ships were therefore found a convenient form of trans-port. The first vessel so used was the CITY OF MEMPHIS which was taken over by General U. S. Grant at Fort Henry in February, 1862.[3] Accord-ing to the Quartermaster General, at one time there were employed "in the transportation of the sick from the Army of the Potomac alone,.... seven powerful steamers and three large sailing ships."[4] Subsequently, a number of other ships were utilized, including several that were sup-plied by the Governors of the Northern States. None of these vessels, however, appears to have been more than a temporary expedient to bring the sick and the wounded to hastily erected hospitals or hospital camps.

---

[3] Percy M. Ashburn, A History of the Medical Department of the United States Army (Boston, 1929), p. 82.

[4] Annual Report, Quartermaster General, 1862, p. 18. As Medical Direc-tor of the Army of the Potomac, the celebrated Dr. Jonathan Letterman devised an evacuation system whereby all wounded men were collected within twenty-hours and placed under shelter.

The War With Spain

At the close of the Civil War further need of hospital vessels
vanished, to reappear again only after the outbreak of hostilities with
Spain in 1898. The Spanish-American War resulted in comparatively few
wounded men, but the many victims of disease, notably typhoid fever,
required extensive hospitalization. Both the Quartermaster General,
who was responsible for the transportation of the sick and wounded,
and the Surgeon General, who was charged with their medical care, were
then totally unprepared for the task at hand. The Surgeon General,
George M. Sternberg, promptly realized the need of a hospital ship,
and late in April 1898 he recommended that the JOHN ENGLIS, a Long Island Sound passenger vessel, be obtained for use as a floating hospital
in the Cuban operations. There was some delay in obtaining necessary
approval from the Quartermaster General, but the vessel was finally purchased on 18 May 1898. After having been provided with the requisite
special equipment and medical supplies, this vessel, renamed the RELIEF,
set sail for Cuba on 2 July, arriving at Siboney some five days later.
On 19 July the RELIEF left Siboney with 254 sick and wounded who were
delivered at New York on 23 July 1898. Subsequently, after the close
of operations in Cuba and Puerto Rico, the vessel gave good service on
a similar mission to the Philippines.

On 1 July 1898, Mr. B. N. Baker, President of the Atlantic Transport Line, tendered the steamship MISSOURI with her captain and crew
to the Federal Government for use as a hospital ship. The offer was
accepted by the Secretary of War and a representative of the Surgeon

General's Office was detailed to prepare the ship for service. But the MISSOURI was only a cattle boat, with no passenger accommodations except quarters for a small crew. New plumbing, ventilation, refrigeration, a steam laundry, an operating room, an X-ray room, laboratories, a new galley, and, of course, wards for patients and the usual medical supplies and equipment had to be provided. By dint of working day and night the vessel was finally made ready to sail for Santiago de Cuba on 23 August.

The MISSOURI and the RELIEF were the only real hospital ships in Army service during the Spanish-American War. Both were comparatively small vessels. The MISSOURI, built in 1889, had a gross tonnage of 2,903 and was 320 feet long, while the RELIEF, built in 1896, was 290.8 feet long and had a gross tonnage of 3,094. Their work, however, was supplemented by the temporary employment of other vessels. Thus, the steamship OLIVETTE, a water carrier, was made a hospital ship by being outfitted with the equipment of a field hospital. The steamers SENECA and CONCHO also were pressed into service, although neither had adequate accommodations. The Massachusetts Volunteer Aid Association supplied a hospital ship, the BAY STATE, which removed 336 patients from Cuba and Puerto Rico. Fortunately the war ended quickly and evacuation by sea never became a major problem.[5]

---

[5] On Army hospital ships in the War with Spain see Report of the Commission Appointed by the President to Investigate the Conduct of the War Department in the War with Spain, vol. 1 (Washington, 1900). pp. 142-43, 717-20. Cf. P. M. Ashburn, op. cit., pp. 198-203. See also the Report of the Surgeon General for the years 1898-1900, passim.

The Protection of Hospital Ships by International Agreement

The protected status of hospital ships may be traced to the efforts of Jean Henri Dunant (1828-1910). Dunant's account of the appalling bloodshed at the battle of Solferino in Italy led to the adoption at an international conference in Switzerland of the first Geneva Convention of 1864, an international agreement whereby protection was accorded to wounded soldiers and to medical personnel under the international symbol of a white flag with a red cross. In subsequent international conferences at Geneva and at The Hague the principles of the initial agreement of 1864 were extended to maritime warfare and in particular to hospital ships. The latter were to be inviolable when operated in accordance with the applicable agreements, and they were to carry distinct marks of identification, such as a green stripe on a white background and a white flag with a red cross. At the Hague Peace Conference of 1899 Great Britain withdrew previous objections to the application to maritime warfare of the Geneva Convention of 1864, and after further revision in 1906 an agreement was finally concluded on 18 October 1907 as Convention X at the Hague Peace Conference of that year.[6] Together with certain other powers the United States was a party to Convention X, which henceforth governed the operation of hospital ships.[7]

---

[6] See James Brown Scott, ed., The Hague Conventions and Declarations of 1899 and 1907 (New York, 1918). See also the helpful compilation by Col. Albert G. Love entitled The Geneva Red Cross Movement, published as No. 62, Army Medical Bulletin, May 1942.

[7] The 28 articles of Convention X are reprinted as Section II of AR 55-130 of 30 December 1943, which relates to Army hospital ships.

World War I

Although the United States hospital ships in operation during the War with Spain had to carry the prescribed markings for protection against attack by surface craft, they were not exposed to the menace of submarine warfare which characterized ocean traffic in World War I. Mindful of this menace, the Surgeon General of the Army, W. C. Gorgas, in a memorandum of 14 November 1917 addressed to the Secretary of War, called attention to the problem of transporting sick and wounded from France to the United States. The Surgeon General proposed that the following classes of patients be evacuated to the United States:

"First: Cases of insanity and tuberculosis.

"Second: Wounded officers and enlisted men who are permanently disabled and who have reached a stage where they would not require active surgical treatment while at sea.

"Third: Officers and enlisted men permanently disabled from disease.

"Fourth: Officers and enlisted men not necessarily permanently disabled from disease or injury but who will probably be under treatment for long periods."

As to means of transportation the Surgeon General suggested two alternatives, namely, returning transports carrying troops and supplies, or regular hospital ships. The former, he believed, would "undoubtedly be liable to destruction by submarines," with a resultant loss of life. As to the latter, it was his belief that "in spite of reports to the contrary ... a hospital ship, traveling openly and marked by day and night, and not suspected of carrying any contrabrand articles, will not be intentionally sunk." He urged, accordingly, that the matter of protection "be taken up by the State Department." The sick and wounded, he declared, were "entitled to every comfort, care, and protection," and it was his opinion that the use of hospital ships should not be abandoned unless the enemy refused to guarantee protection or showed "some specific hostile intention." Lastly the Surgeon General recommended that "the question of allotting a certain number of ships for use as hospital ships be considered, so that they may be properly prepared, or, in the event of a decision to the contrary, that the details of regulations for carrying sick and wounded on transports may be completed."[8]

The recommendation of the Surgeon General passed through the usual round of indorsements and memoranda but resulted in no Army hospital ships, principally because of the acute shortage of shipping and because of the belief expressed by the Chief of Embarkation Service that the sick and wounded should be evacuated on hospital ships and transports under the control of the Navy. As of January 1918 the Navy had in actual service only one hospital ship, the SOLACE, a veteran of the War with Spain, although two other hospital ships were under construction. Consequently, the Navy Department was ill equipped to handle the needs of all the armed services. Nevertheless, by agreement of 28 March 1918 between the War and the Navy Department, the following policy was adopted with respect to the evacuation by sea of sick and wounded personnel:

"(a) Sick and wounded being brought from France or England to the United States will be brought in Navy hospital ships or transports, whichever may be most suitable and available, except in special cases where transportation by commercial liners may be authorized.

---

[8] The Medical Department of the United States Army in the World War, The Surgeon General's Office, vol. I (Washington, D. C., 1923), p. 359. For copies of the pertinent correspondence and agreements see pp. 358-70.

"(b) The Army will be in charge of the embarkation and debarkation of all Army patients.

"(c) The Navy will be charged with the care of these patients while on board ships of the Navy acting as transports or otherwise. At the request of the Navy, the Army will render such assistance in personnel and material as may be necessary."

"(d) No patients will be returned to the United States if, in the opinion of the Surgeons concerned, they will probably recover within six months."

On 13 August 1918 the Surgeon General withdrew the various requests previously made by him for hospital or ambulance ships to be operated under his jurisdiction. By first indorsement of 11 September 1918, in response to a query from the Army Chief of Staff, the Surgeon General called attention to the agreement of 28 March 1918, under which the Navy was charged with the return of patients from overseas forces. The Surgeon General, however, favored special hospital ships and did "not acquiesce in the idea of removing the sick and wounded returning from France completely from the protection that might be afforded them under the Geneva Convention."

For the most part, during World War I Army patients were returned on transports under the jurisdiction of the Navy, which also carried returning troops. Fortunately American participation in the conflict was comparatively short-lived, and the armistice of 11 November 1918 was signed before it became necessary to bring back a large number of patients from abroad. Since there were adequate hospital facilities in France and England for the American patients on hand, no difficulty was had in returning the sick and wounded on regular transports, where they could be distributed over as long a period as proved necessary.[9]

---

[9] Ibid., vol. 1, pp. 370-71.

II

EVACUATION OF SICK AND WOUNDED ARMY PERSONNEL

The acquisition by the United States of the Atlantic bases in September 1940 gave rise to a demand for proper hospital facilities to be "permanently installed on troop transports to care for the evacuation of sick." In a memorandum of 4 November 1940 the Acting Assistant Chief of Staff, G-4, described the providing of such facilities as "a vital morale and political consideration in any initial occupation of the recently acquired bases ... where general hospital facilities will not be available for some time to come." The same source revealed a plan to utilize eventually either the CHATEAU THIERRY or the ST. MIHIEL "as a full hospital ship," such use having already been contemplated in the 1942 estimates of the Quartermaster General.

Inception of Hospital Ship Program

The rapid expansion of the Army Transport Service in 1940-41 led to the taking over of many vessels as transports, upon which hospital space was either inadequate or non-existent. The need of providing suitable hospital areas and the requisite medical detachments on board such ships placed a particularly heavy burden upon the Port Surgeon at the New York Port of Embarkation.[10] Evidently as the result of this development, the Port Surgeon at New York, the late Col. (then Lt. Col.) Louis A. Milne, was among the "first to recognize the growing need ... of

---

[10] See Historical Report of the Port Surgeon, New York Port of Embarkation, 4 August 1942.

hospital ships to be operated by the Army." As early as 1940 he appears to have envisaged Army hospital ships, and although "his untiring efforts" to that end were interrupted by his death in 1943, the Deputy Surgeon General, Major General George F. Lull, subsequently stated that Col. Milne's work "laid the foundation for the present hospital ship program." In fitting recognition of Col. Milne's "pioneer role" in the development of the Army hospital fleet the former SS LEWIS LUCKENBACH (now undergoing conversion at Boston) was renamed the USAHS LOUIS A. MILNE in July 1944.[11]

Army versus Navy Operation

As previously indicated, during World War I the Navy took charge of the return of the sick and wounded to the United States. During the spring of 1941 when it seemed likely that all the Army transports, including the hospital facilities on board, would be placed under the control of the Navy, Lt. Col. Milne became "quite exercised over the matter," advancing many arguments against such a transfer. Col. Milne's objections to control by the Navy were supported by the experience in World War I of the Medical Department of the Port of Embarkation at Hoboken, New Jersey, where one of the lessons learned was "that a satisfactory medical service cannot be established or maintained on a transport not wholly under the control of the Army." In May 1941 Lt. Col. Milne managed to make his sentiments known to Lt. Col. Frank S. Ross,

---

[11] See memorandum of 3 July 1944 from the Deputy Surgeon General to the Chief of Transportation.

then with G-4 in Washington. But so far as is known no further action was taken at that time.[12]

On 29 October 1941 the Port Surgeon of the New York Port of Embarkation proposed the development of a hospital ship for the Army Transport Service. By second indorsement of 24 November 1941 the Surgeon General requested information as to the contemplated policy in regard to evacuation of sick and injured from overseas garrisons, and asked whether such evacuation was to be a responsibility of the Army or the Navy. Before any further determination of policy could be obtained, the United States was plunged into war. But even under wartime conditions the Navy apparently still was thought of as the primary means of evacuating the sick and wounded from overseas areas.

On 8 December 1941 the Assistant Chief of Staff, G-4, Brig. Gen. Brehon Somervell, took action to secure basic information on the evacuation of patients from all Atlantic bases, with a view to determining the necessity for a hospital ship. Upon receipt of the desired data, such action as was deemed necessary would, it was noted, involve, first, asking the Navy Department if it could handle the situation; second, if the Navy could not do so, requesting a ship from the Maritime Commission; and, as a last resort, submitting the problem to the Joint Board.[13] Available files do not reveal what information was actually developed.[14] But

---

[12] See unsigned note of 24 May 1941 to Lt. Col. Frank S. Ross with attached copy of the annual report of the Medical Department at Hoboken for the fiscal year 1919.

[13] See G-4/29717, "For record only."

[14] AG 573.27, which contains the basic correspondence, is missing from the AGO files.

according to Lt. Col. John C. Fitzpatrick of the Office of the Surgeon General, the total estimated number of evacuees was not large and their locations were so scattered as to make impracticable the use of a hospital ship. Apparently not until May 1943, when the shipping crisis had eased and the North African campaign had begun to swell the Army casualty lists, did the War Department determine to have its own fleet of hospital ships.

Recommendations of the Surgeon General and the Quartermaster General

If there was to be a fleet of Army hospital ships, the task of procuring, converting, equipping, and manning the necessary vessels would have to be accomplished under the direction of the Surgeon General and of the Quartermaster General. Early in January 1942, in cooperation with the Transportation Branch, G-4, representatives of both the Surgeon General and the Quartermaster General conferred on the subject with a view to obtaining certain special ships to augment the hospital facilities of the regular transports. At a conference held in Washington, D. C., on 2 January 1942, there was discussed the possibility of obtaining either Red Cross hospital ships—provided that immunity from destruction could be secured from the enemy—or the so-called ambulance transports that could bring back patients on the homeward passage. Specifically, the steamers FLORIDA and SHAWNEE were suggested for possible use because of their "large stateroom capacity and public rooms which could be converted into operating rooms and general wards, giving a very large capacity for hospitalized troops."[15] Following this conference, by memorandum for the

---

[15] Memorandum of Mr. G. A. Anthony to Col. C. H. Kells, 3 January 1942. Mr. Anthony represented the Office of the Quartermaster General at the conference.

Assistant Chief of Staff, G-4, dated 5 January 1942, the Office of the Surgeon General recommended:

1.   That two hospital ships be provided for the evacuation of sick and wounded, one based on the East Coast and the other on the West Coast.

2.   That Army transports be fitted for conversion on return trips to carry sick and wounded, with ample hospital accommodations to provide nursing attention and emergency service for medical and surgical conditions that might develop en route.

Provision also was made in the Supplemental Estimates "D" of the War Department for the fiscal year 1942 for six hospital ships to cost $6,000,000 each. The Quartermaster General attempted "to assure immediate delivery of one hospital ship for the Atlantic and one for the Pacific," with later deliveries of four C3 type vessels from the Maritime Commission. The Superintendent of the Army Transport Service at New York, Col. Hans Ottzenn, advised informally that it was impracticable to convert all Army transports to evacuate sick and wounded from overseas bases. He stated, however, that hospital facilities would be provided commensurate with the troop capacities of the Army transports. As the result of the foregoing discussions, in which the Port Surgeon at New York also participated, the groundwork was laid as early as January 1942 for the development of Army hospital ships and additional hospital facilities on the Army transports.[16]

Regardless of how desirable Army hospital ships might be in the spring of 1942, all plans to that end were blocked out by the prevailing

---

[16]   See "For the Record," G-4/29717-100. Possibly through the influence of the Port Surgeon at New York, Army hospital ship plans were based in part upon the alleged failure of the Navy to meet its responsibility in World War I with respect to the evacuation of Army sick and wounded.

shipping shortage. On 14 February 1942 the Quartermaster General recommended that two ships be laid up for sixty days for conversion at $150,000 each to provide hospital space for use in evacuating sick and wounded from overseas theaters. On 23 February 1942 the Assistant Chief of Staff, G-4, General Somervell, refused to approve this recommendation and requested that the Quartermaster General and the Surgeon General resort to "temporary expedients" and the employment of existing transports during the "present acute shortage of water transportation." Again, as in World War I, the shipping shortage prevented, temporarily at least, the establishment during World War II of a fleet of Army hospital ships.

The Viewpoint of the Maritime Commission

For hospital ships as well as for vessels in general the prime source in 1942 was the Maritime Commission. When the above-mentioned Army item covering the procurement of six hospital ships reached the Bureau of the Budget, Admiral Emory S. Land stated that the Maritime Commission "would procure, build, or charter any ship required by the War Department." As a result this item was disallowed. But the Maritime Commission was "agreeable to adapting six vessels, now planned for construction, for use as hospital ships." Accordingly, on 12 February 1942 Admiral Land as Chairman of the Maritime Commission was requested by the Army Chief of Staff to convert six vessels for hospital purposes.

On 24 February 1942 Admiral Land replied, advancing the viewpoint that "hospital ships fell properly under the cognizance of the Navy Department." To this statement under date of 7 March 1942 the Chief of the Transportation Branch, G-4, Col. C. P. Gross, took vigorous exception.

- 14 -

"The hospital ships requested," said Col. Gross, "will be utilized for the evacuation of Army sick and wounded. A large portion of their crew must necessarily be members of the Army Medical Corps. Their use should be governed by the requirements of The Surgeon General of the Army and their control vested in the War Department."

Possibly because of the continuing extreme scarcity of shipping, Admiral Land refused to approve the plans of the War Department. It was necessary, therefore, to exert additional pressure upon the Maritime Commission. On 1 May 1942 in a letter to Admiral Emory S. Land, Chairman, U. S. Maritime Commission, the Secretary of War stressed the grave need of providing adequately for the evacuation of the sick and wounded from overseas operations. The Secretary also noted that necessary action was being initiated to coordinate Army and Navy operational procedures. On 4 May 1942 Admiral Land replied to the effect that agreement between the War Department and the Navy Department on strategic requirements must precede the allocation of hospital ships. On 29 June 1942, pursuant to a recommendation of the Joint Planners, the Joint Chiefs of Staff approved the following action:

> "That the Maritime Commission be directed through the Navy Department, to acquire for the Army initially three (3) ships to be fitted out as hospital ships according to the specifications prescribed by the Army."

Finally, on 16 July 1942 the Secretary of War formally advised Admiral Land of the above action taken by the Joint Chiefs of Staff.[17]

The First Allocated Hulls for Hospital Ships

In accordance with the above-noted decision of the Joint Chiefs of Staff three hulls were to be acquired and fitted out as hospital ships for Army use

---

[17] For details see G-4/33006-4 and AG 322.15, Hospital Ships.

At first the use of EC2 (Liberty) hulls was contemplated, but this plan
was discarded because the Liberty type is a single compartment vessel.
Subsequently, in September 1942 the Navy was persuaded to give up three
Maritime Commission CIB type hulls, thus providing a two-compartment
ship—an important safety factor in a vessel of this character. In the
fall of 1942 Mr. P. H. Thearle of the Water Division, OCT, prepared the
preliminary plans for the conversion at the New York office of Cox and
Stevens, the facilities of this firm being utilized as an emergency mea-
sure. In a letter of October 22, 1942, Mr. Thearle stated that the plans
had been completed and that the specifications were then under preparation. "The big catch in the whole deal," he added, "is that the Navy
is to accomplish the conversion to our plans and specifications, which
leads us to wonder how long it will take to get them in service."

Mr. Thearle had reason to wonder, since many months elapsed before
any work was ever done on the three allocated hulls, to which the Navy
ultimately assigned the names, COMFORT, HOPE, and MERCY. As planned,
these vessels when converted into hospital ships were to be manned in
the operating departments by the Navy, but the medical personnel was
to be supplied by the Surgeon General of the Army. Proposed patient
capacity of each was 705. Conversion which was accomplished on the
West Coast under Navy contracts, was not begun until June 1943 for the
COMFORT and the MERCY and August 1943 for the HOPE. None of these vessels was actually placed in service until 1944. The COMFORT was completed on 29 April, the MERCY on 7 August and the HOPE on 15 August 1944.[18]

----

[18]   These three vessels were based on the Los Angeles Port of Embarkation
       and were engaged exclusively in operations in the Pacific.

In the meantime, while the Navy Department delayed in providing hospital ships for Army use, the North African and Italian campaigns of 1942-43 with the inevitable casualties resulting therefrom made imperative a reappraisal of the hospital ship program of the War Department.

Evacuation Procedure in 1942

Pending the procurement of regular hospital ships for this purpose, most Army patients in 1942 were, perforce, evacuated from overseas areas by means of hospital spaces available on returning Army vessels. The emphasis at this time was placed on getting troops overseas rather than on bringing back casualties. As already indicated, the determining factor in the 1942 plans for sea evacuation was the prevailing shortage of shipping. By decision JCS 52, dated 21 May 1942, the Joint Chiefs of Staff frankly recognized the current situation by approving the recommendation "that for economy in shipping when there is more or less continuous transport service to an area, evacuation of sick and wounded be normally accomplished by returning transports."[19] Certain other means of evacuation also were explored in 1942, such as the possible use of an ambulance transport;[20] the suggested provision of additional hospital space on certain British vessels;[21] and, finally, evacuation by

---

[19] Cf. Memorandum of 26 September 1942 from Maj. Francis Lee to Col. Connor, subject, "Hospital Ships."

[20] An ambulance transport carries troops outbound and patients inbound, but has no protected status.

[21] Notably, the QUEEN MARY and the QUEEN ELIZABETH. At the close of 1944 this project was still under consideration.

air.[22]

On 18 June 1942 the Commanding General, Services of Supply, was charged with "administrative responsibility for the coordination of the plans of all commands for the evacuation of the sick and wounded to be delivered to his control, and for coordination of plans for hospitalization within the continental United States."[23] In September 1942 the Adjutant General issued a directive requiring overseas commanders to supply certain essential information concerning the evacuation of sick and wounded from overseas.[24] The requirement was met in two reports: one, a monthly report indicating the number of patients actually awaiting evacuation from overseas, and the number of additional patients anticipated within the next thirty days; the other, a special report to be submitted by the overseas commander upon the sailing of any vessel with patients being evacuated to the United States. By November 1942 this system of reporting had resulted in a "reasonably correct picture of the current status of hospitalization and evacuation" of the armed forces, thereby making it possible to estimate the ship facilities re-

---

[22] At a conference of 7 November 1942, attended by representatives of the Chief of Transportation, the Surgeon General, the Air Surgeon, the Air Transport Command, and Headquarters, Services of Supply, the groundwork was laid for the use of air transportation to evacuate Army patients from overseas areas.

[23] AG 704 (6-17-42) MB-D-TS-M, June 18, 1942, subject: "War Department Hospitalization and Evacuation Policy."

[24] AG 370.5 (9-15-42) MS-SPOPH-M, September 16, 1942, subject: "Essential Information Concerning the Evacuation of Sick and Wounded from Overseas."

quired for evacuation.[25] Also in the fall of 1942 the Commanding Officers of the Army Ports of Embarkation were made responsible for evacuation to the zone of the interior of sick and wounded personnel returned from the overseas forces maintained by their respective ports.[26]

The Determination of Requirements

In order to determine the necessary shipping space, the Surgeon General's Office had to estimate what the overall requirements would be with respect to evacuation of the sick and wounded from overseas in World War II. This was not an easy problem to solve. The Army was operating in many areas where it had never operated before; combat methods had changed since World War I; and it was extremely difficult to estimate how many casualties would result from a given campaign. Nevertheless, on the basis of comprehensive studies of battle casualty statistics of World War I and estimates prepared by the Office of the Surgeon General as to the incidence of disease and non-battle injuries in the overseas areas, anticipated rates of evacuation were arrived at, which, when applied against projected troop deployment throughout the world, resulted in an approximate monthly rate of evacuation of sick and wounded to the United States. The precise estimates have not been revealed, but evidently

---

[25] See Memorandum for General Le R. Lutes, dated 17 November 1942, from Col. W. L. Wilson, Chief, Hospitalization and Evacuation Branch, Plans Division, Operations, SOS.

[26] W. D. Letter, Services of Supply, SPOPM-322.15, September 15, 1942, subject, "Operation Plans for Military Hospitalization and Evacuation."

they proved conservative.[27]

Fortunately, after the inception late in 1942 of monthly reports from the overseas theaters, estimates made in Washington could be corrected on the basis of the actual number of patients awaiting evacuation overseas. Specifically, at this time the Office of the Surgeon General planned that approximately 40 per cent, or the so-called "helpless" portion of the total number of Army patients would be evacuated by sea in convention-protected hospital ships. The remainder, approximately 60 per cent, would be removed on returning troop transports.

The two hospital ships (the RELIEF and the SOLACE) which the Navy had in 1942 were fully occupied with current operations in the Pacific. For pending operations in the Atlantic the Army therefore had to rely upon its own resources. No doubt with this contingency in mind, on 11 August 1942, the Commanding General in the European Theater of Operations advised the War Department at Washington that it was his policy to evacuate helpless patients "only on plainly marked and regularly operated hospital ships." The estimates of casualties from his theater, he added, would require five hospital ships prior to 1 April 1943.

Subsequently, after the landings had been made by United States forces in North Africa, it was found possible to utilize British hospital ships for evacuation to the United Kingdom. Nevertheless, under date of 27 March 1943 the Commanding General, North African Theater, notified the

_____

[27]   See the remarks of Lt. Col. John C. Fitzpatrick of the Surgeon General's Office at the Conference of Port Surgeons and Troop Movement Officers, Fort Hamilton, New York, 13 October, 1943, on pp. 73-74 of the processed proceedings.

War Department of "an increase in requirements for sea evacuation of patients" and requested "two United States (convention-protected) hospital ships."

III

THE FIRST ARMY HOSPITAL SHIP IN WORLD WAR II

During the spring of 1943 the shipping situation gradually improved, as means were devised to cope with enemy submarines and as additional vessels were turned out in American yards. Moreover, it became increasingly apparent that the enemy was disposed to respect convention-protected hospital ships.[28] Under these circumstances the Office of the Surgeon General recommended in March 1943 that regular convention-protected hospital ships be considered the normal resource for evacuating the helpless portion (an estimated 40 per cent) of the sick and wounded. Nevertheless, the shipping situation was still so tight that no hospital ship space could be released until adequate assurance was given that the current troop lift would not be disturbed.

The ACADIA as an Ambulance Transport

The necessity of avoiding any reduction in the current troop lift was the chief consideration underlying the initial decision in 1942 to employ the ACADIA as an ambulance transport, that is, to carry troops outbound and to return patients inbound. During the planning of the North African operations General Eisenhower repeatedly called attention to the need for Army hospital ships. Thus on 21 August 1942 he reported to the Adjutant General at Washington that three 500-bed hospital ships

---

[28] Inquiry made as early as in May and again in August 1942 disclosed no deliberate violation of the Geneva Convention by the enemy. Cf. Memorandum of Lt. Col. W. L. Wilson for Col. B. M. Harloe, 22 May 1942; and document M.02926/42, dated 11 March 1942, forwarded to the Adjutant General on 22 August 1942 by Brig. Gen. J. E. Dahlquist, AG 560-G.

U. S. ARMY HOSPITAL SHIP ACADIA

This was the first officially recognized United States
Army hospital ship in the present war

would be required by late September and that modified passenger vessels would be acceptable. The acute shipping shortage, however, made it clear that no Army hospital ships could be provided in the early stages of the North African campaign and that the ACADIA could not be used as an ambulance transport until about D30 or 40.[29]

A steel vessel of 6,185 gross tons, the ACADIA was built in 1932 at Newport News, Virginia. On 25 November 1941 she was obtained by the Army on time charter. After hasty conversion into an Army transport at New York she left that port (Voyage No. 1) on 20 December 1941 bound for Balboa, Canal Zone, via New Orleans. Subsequently, in the spring of 1942 the ACADIA made a number of voyages in the Caribbean area before being transferred to Boston to be converted into an ambulance transport.

On 20 August 1942, while the conversion was still in progress, Col. C. H. Kells, Executive of the Water Division, OCT, requested that the War Shipping Administration confirm the previous oral arrangements whereby the ACADIA had been made available to the Army on a bareboat basis. After a condition survey of 2 October 1942 at East Boston, Massachusetts, the S. S. ACADIA was redelivered on 16 October 1942 to the War Shipping Administration and simultaneously delivered by that agency to the War Department under sub-bareboat charter.

The object of the conversion at Boston, which was accomplished in the summer and fall of 1942, was not to produce a hospital ship per se but simply an Army transport so equipped that a minimum of the troop-

---

[29]
    See Memorandum of 26 September 1942 from Maj. Francis Lee to Col. Connor, subject "Hospital Ships."

carrying capacity was lost while providing an approximate 500-patient capacity on return trips.[30]   The actual conversion was begun on 11 June and was completed on 16 October 1942.   The vessel arrived at New York on 17 October 1942 and was inspected by the Port Surgeon, Col. L. A. Milne. Colonel Milne thought of the ACADIA as "an experiment in trying to operate a troop ship and a five hundred bed Hospital Ship at the same time." It was, therefore, his opinion that only experience would disclose the necessary changes and adjustments.   But he did note that the available quarters on board were inadequate for both the nurses and the enlisted personnel.   Subsequently, additional work had to be performed at New York and the vessel was not ready until 4 December 1942.[31]   Necessary repairs and extensive alterations, together with armament and degaussing, resulted in a total expenditure of some $1,300,000 for the conversion proper.

During the period from December 1942 to April 1943 the ACADIA made several voyages between New York and North Africa, sailing in convoy and carrying troops outbound and military casualties inbound.   But by March 1943 the urgent need of hospital ships in the North African theater led to the demand for a change in the status of this vessel.   Particularly revealing as to the emergency in North Africa was the voyage report dated 11 March 1943 of the Surgeon aboard the ACADIA, in which he described the prevailing conditions upon his arrival at Oran on 21 February 1943.

---

[30] See Memorandum of 24 June 1942 from Col. E. McGinley to General Lutes.

[31] Among other changes, hydrotherapeutic equipment was not installed in order to provide additional hospital space. See File 444.3 "Army Transports," for basic communication of 15 October 1942 from Col. D. C. Watkins, OCT, to the Surgeon General, and the first, second, and third indorsements.

"All of the hospitals in the area were," he said, "full and overflowing with patients and wounded." Furthermore, "there was dire need for evacuation of a great many of these men to relieve the congestion of hospitals and to make more room for the wounded coming in hourly." Yet it was decided at Oran that only ambulatory patients could be removed on the ACADIA to the United States. As a result "this excellently equipped ship had to return practically empty," despite the presence of trained personnel (the 204th Hospital Ship Company) to care for a full load of the sick and the wounded. Lastly, the Surgeon noted that the hospitals in North Africa were "in great need of supplies" which might well be brought on the ACADIA without violating any treaties. Instead of being used, his personnel, he lamented, were "traveling needlessly back and forth on what might be called a pleasure cruise."

On 30 March 1943 in a memorandum to the Operations Division of the General Staff, Brig. Gen. L. B. McAfee of the Surgeon General's Office called attention to a recent decision of the Judge Advocate General indicating that hospital ships might be utilized to transport medical personnel, equipment and supplies to overseas bases. At the same time General McAfee noted that Germany and her allies were evidently disposed to recognize registered hospital ships. He recommended, accordingly, that the ACADIA "be immediately registered as a hospital ship under the provisions of the Geneva Convention, and that this ship be utilized to carry medical supplies and medical personnel to theaters of war and to return sick and wounded therefrom to the United States."

At a conference of 12 April 1943 attended by representatives of the Chief of Transportation (Brig. Gen. R. H. Wylie, Lt. Col. D. E. Farr,

Maj. J. A. Griffin), of the Surgeon General, and of the Planning Division, ASF, it was decided that the basic problem with respect to hospital ships was to secure amendment of the current sea evacuation policy, as determined by Item 2, 16th Meeting, 25 May 1942, of the Joint Chiefs of Staff, whereby returning troop transports were designated as the primary means of such evacuation. As amended, the policy was to have convention-protected hospital ships declared "the normal means, when available, of evacuating the helpless fraction of the sick and wounded."[32] More specifically, the conferees questioned the "current use" of the USAT ACADIA "in view of the resulting concentration of sick and wounded on an enemy target," and recommended therefore the immediate registration of the vessel as a convention-protected hospital ship.

Designation of ACADIA as an Army Hospital Ship

By April 1943 it had become evident that the ACADIA could be operated more safely and expeditiously for evacuation of the sick and wounded if declared a regular hospital ship rather than allowed to continue in service as an ambulance transport.[33] Accordingly, with the approval of the Chief of Transportation, on 24 April 1943, the Chief of the Water Division instructed the Ship Operations Branch to arrange for the registration of the ACADIA as a convention-protected hospital ship. The ACADIA

---

[32] See Memorandum of 24 April 1943 from Lt. Gen. Brehon Somervell to the Assistant Chief of Staff, Operations Division.

[33] The decision to register the ACADIA as an Army hospital ship was evidently influenced by the experience of our British allies who had operated several hospital ships in the Atlantic and in the Mediterranean with full immunity. Cf. the lecture by Capt. A. S. Rogoff at the Atlantic Coast Transportation Corps Officers Training School on the "Operation of Hospital Trains and Hospital Ships in Evacuation of Sick and Wounded (n.d., Restricted), p. 4.

was already earmarked for the North African theater, in compliance with a request of 12 April 1943 from the Commanding General that the vessel "be allocated to NATOUSA when available."

The decision to employ the ACADIA as a regular hospital ship necessitated a secondary conversion which was accomplished at New York during the period April-June 1943. This was a comparatively simple job involving chiefly the removal of armament and other belligerent features. The entire hull was painted white, a horizontal green band was painted on the whole length of each side, and the usual red crosses on the sides, deck and funnel, which could be illuminated at night, were also provided. In short, the mission of the vessel was clearly indicated by the use of the distinguishing marks prescribed under international practice.

Because the ACADIA was the first hospital ship to be placed in operation by the Army since the War with Spain, precedents for its designation as such by the War Department were practically non-existent. The Navy, however, had just placed the hospital ship RELIEF in service and was therefore able to furnish helpful information on the procedure to be followed. The primary step consisted of a formal letter from the Secretary of War to the Secretary of State designating the USAT ACADIA as a hospital ship, describing its physical characteristics and marks of identification, and requesting that the proper notification be made through the appropriate channels to all the enemy governments. Through the American Legation at Bern the State Department next requested the Swiss Government to notify all enemy governments of the designation of the ACADIA as a hospital ship.

On 6 May 1943 the Secretary of War gave formal notice to the Secretary of State of the designation of the ACADIA, and one week later, by cable, the State Department notified the Swiss Government at Bern. On 17 May via Bern the Hungarian, Bulgarian, Rumanian, Italian and German Governments were notified and on 18 May the Japanese Government was also notified concerning the ACADIA. Following the example set by the Navy Department, the War Department allowed approximately two weeks to elapse between the time notification was made to the enemy and the actual dispatching of the vessel, which in this instance was scheduled to sail on 31 May. Finally by War Department General Order No. 27, 3 June 1943, the ACADIA was officially designated as a United States Army hospital ship.

The above-outlined procedure set the pattern of designation and notification for all the other vessels which subsequently were added to the Army's fleet of hospital ships.[34]

The Maiden Voyage of the USAHS ACADIA

On 5 June 1943 the Army hospital ship ACADIA sailed from New York on her maiden voyage to Oran. She arrived at that port on 14 June, left two days later, and reached New York on 25 June 1943. On the return voyage the vessel carried 749 Army and 29 Navy patients. The Army patients, all of whom were evacuated and delivered to the Halloran General Hospital, consisted of 195 medical, 295 surgical, and 259 neuropsychiatric cases. Evacuation was somewhat delayed by the inability of the hospital to receive ambulant patients as rapidly as it was possible to deliver them

---

[34] The process of designation was developed throughout by the Ship Operations Branch, Water Division, OCT.

from the ship.

Special attention was paid to the debarkation of the ACADIA at
New York on 25 June 1943. The band of Fort Hamilton was on hand to add
cheer to the reception, and representatives of the American Red Cross
dispensed orange juice, sandwiches, cigarettes and chewing gum. A Sena-
tor and a Congressman were also present. The Surgeon General of the
Army, the Chief of Transportation, and the Commanding General of the
New York Port of Embarkation headed the inspection party which boarded
the vessel immediately upon arrival at the pier. As was to be expected,
the inspection disclosed the need of certain corrective measures which
ultimately were accomplished through the Port Surgeon at New York, Col.
H. R. Melton.

By letter of 26 June 1943 the Chief of Transportation, Major General
Gross, advised Major General Groninger, Commanding General, New York Port
of Embarkation, that he and the Surgeon General (Major General Kirk) both
felt "that there was something wanting on the ACADIA." In particular it
was noted that the nurses wore regular working slacks that varied in
color and quality. Also, many of the patients were badly in need of haircuts and shaves. The matter of the slacks was immediately taken up with
the Office of the Surgeon General which arranged to have suitable standard
slacks manufactured and issued so that the nurses would present a uniform
appearance. As for the patients, a barber shop was established aboard
the ACADIA to provide needed haircuts and shaves. Lastly, on 26 June
1943 Lt. Col. John C. Fitzpatrick, an experienced transport surgeon, was
sent to New York to advise and assist the Port Surgeon and the Commanding

Officer of the USAHS ACADIA in improving the general administration of the vessel.

On 2 July 1943 Major General Groninger forwarded to Major General Gross a complete report on the debarkation of the ACADIA, at the same time giving assurance that the "unsatisfactory conditions" which had been noticed would receive his "continued personal attention." On 28 June the ACADIA again sailed for Oran. The vessel continued in regular service in the Mediterranean area throughout the remainder of 1943.

IV

THE ARMY HOSPITAL SHIP PROGRAM, 1943-44

Throughout 1942 and well into 1943, the shipping shortage effectively prevented the allocation of even a single vessel to serve as a convention-protected Army hospital ship. Hospital spaces on Army transports and a number of British hospital ships were accordingly utilized to evacuate the casualties of the North African campaign. Both the Surgeon General and the Chief of Transportation were aware of the grave hazards involved in transporting Army patients on vessels subject to attack by the enemy, and both realized that a storm of public criticism was bound to arise if American lives were lost because of this type of evacuation. Yet all considerations, moral as well as humanitarian, were overshadowed by the impelling need of using every foot of available space to carry combat units overseas. But by the spring of 1943 such arrangements had proved inadequate, and as a result first, the ACADIA, and next the SEMINOLE were hastily put into operation as convention-protected Army hospital ships.

The USAHS SEMINOLE

The SEMINOLE, a combination steel vessel with a gross tonnage of 5,896, built at Newport News in 1925, was purchased for Army use on 22 May 1943. Despite "a small potential patient capacity (180-bed, 150 other probable)," on 11 May 1943, in view of the "time requirements" it was decided that this vessel should be converted to a convention-protected hospital ship.[35] Conversion, which was done in great haste, was accomplished at New York "on an around-the-clock basis," at a total cost of $1,249,970.51. On 8 May 1943 the SEMINOLE was officially designated as an Army hospital ship. The same procedure in designation was followed as had been established for the ACADIA. But in order to give both vessels a more official character, it was found advisable in the summer of 1943 to provide each ship with a certificate of commission, an impressive document signed and sealed by both the Secretary of War and the Secretary of State, officially identifying her as an Army hospital ship.[36]

Like the ACADIA, the SEMINOLE was employed throughout late 1943 to evacuate sick and wounded in the Mediterranean area. Running on a shuttle basis, the vessel evacuated casualties from the military operations on Sicily and on the Italian mainland. On 5 November 1943 while the SEMINOLE was at Naples, enemy aircraft dropped bombs which exploded some 200 feet from the vessel but resulted in no casualties.[37]

---

[35] See Diary of Chief of Zone of Interior Branch for 11 May 1943, Hospitalization and Evacuation Section, which states that the decision was reached by Brig. Gen. R. H. Wylie, Lt. Col. R. D. Meyer and Lt. Col. D. E. Farr of the Office of the Chief of Transportation.

[36] This was done at the suggestion of Major William Lepski of the New York Port of Embarkation who recommended on 26 June 1943 that Army hospital ships be furnished with a more formidable document than a printed copy of the General Order designating the vessel as a U. S. Army Hospital Ship.

[37] In a dispatch from Naples of 27 April 1944, the ubiquitous Ernie Pyle mentioned the SEMINOLE with its lights, clean beds, and hot water as being the nearest thing to peacetime that he had ever seen in a war zone.

The ACADIA and the SEMINOLE were soon to be joined by other vessels in the rapidly expanding Army hospital fleet.

Scope of the Army Hospital Ship Program

In a conference of 12 April 1943[38] that preceded the designation of the ACADIA as the first Army hospital ship, consideration had also been given to the conversion of other vessels, either passenger-type ships or the so-called EC2 or Liberty type cargo vessels. Of the latter type it was then suggested that six hulls might be procured, converted and registered as hospital ships. The Army still counted upon the three hospital ships which were to be converted by the Navy. But although the Chief of Transportation had urgently recommended that these three ships be available to sail by 30 September 1942, the actual conversions by the Navy did not begin until the summer of 1943. Obviously many more months must elapse before the Navy could deliver a completed vessel.

At this same conference it was also noted that the basic problem in enlarging the Army hospital fleet was to secure the amendment of the current sea evacuation policy which contemplated the employment of returning troop transports as the chief means of evacuating the sick and the wounded. Through appropriate channels (Lt. Gen. Somervell) the proposed amendment, whereby convention-protected hospital ships would be designated the normal means of evacuating the so-called "helpless fraction of the

----

[38] Held at Washington, D. C., this conference on hospital ships was attended by representatives of the Chief of Transportation, the Surgeon General, and the Planning Division, ASF.

sick and wounded," was ultimately brought before the Joint Staff Planners. On 30 May 1943 the latter submitted their report on hospital
ships to the Joint Chiefs of Staff, with the following recommendations:

      a.   An amendment stating that the helpless fraction of
the sick and wounded be evacuated by convention-protected hospital ships, when available.

      b.   A conversion program limiting the type of vessels to
slow-speed passenger vessels and/or EC-2 cargo ships. The conversion program outlines the conversion of ships to a total of
15 ships by December 31, 1943, 19 ships by June 30, 1944, and
24 ships by December 31, 1944.

      c.   Preparation by the Army to convert, crew, staff, and
operate the required number of hospital ships.

      d.   Authority for the Army to convert cargo ships to
troop carriers in proportion to the troop lift lost through
conversion of passenger ships to hospital ships.

      e.   Limitation of the outbound use of convention-pro-
tected hospital ships to the transportation of medical personnel and supplies.

The Joint Chiefs of Staff on 11 June 1943 approved the recommendations of the Joint Staff Planners and requested that appropriate action
be taken to effect the necessary implementation. By memorandum of 18
June 1943 Maj. Gen. LeR. Lutes, Director of Operations, ASF, informed
the Chief of Transportation of the aforementioned decision, requested
that the necessary measures be taken. and authorized direct communication thereon with the Surgeon General. The scope of the Army hospital
ship program was at last determined. All told it was to cover 24 ships,
including, however, the three vessels already under conversion by the
Navy.

Types of Vessels Used

In 1943 ships were still at a premium and the Army consequently had little choice in the vessels available for conversion into hospital ships. Moreover, any troop lift lost through the conversion of passenger vessels to hospital ships had to be made up by the conversion of cargo ships to troop carriers. Special construction, of course, was out of the question. Under these circumstances the Army simply had to take what it could get. There was no compelling reason why a hospital ship should be built from the bottom up, and in consequence all the vessels ultimately obtained by the Army for this purpose represented conversion of completed craft of varying ages and types.[39] Moreover, since speed was no objective, the tendency was to convert into Army hospital ships various older vessels that had proved too slow for convoy use.

The Joint Chiefs of Staff had, in fact, limited the conversion program to "slow-speed passenger vessels and/or EC2 cargo ships." As already indicated, for a time the use of EC2 vessels, or the so-called Liberty ships, was contemplated, but the Navy had objected. As a result no such vessels were selected for conversion into Army hospital ships until late in 1943. Slow-speed passenger vessels, then, remained the sole source for conversions in the spring and summer of 1943.

By June 1943 some ten vessels had been suggested for possible conversion into Army hospital ships. Of these ten, the oldest was the

---

[39] The three hospital ships obtained through the Navy (the COMFORT, HOPE, and MERCY) were converted directly from C1B hulls allocated by the Maritime Commission.

AGWILEON (ex-YUCATAN, ex-HAVANA, ex-COMFORT), built at Philadelphia in 1907 by William Cramp and Sons. After a checkered career which included a sinking in the East River, the vessel was obtained on a bareboat basis for the Army by the War Shipping Administration on 27 November 1942. Next in point of age were the ERNEST HINDS (ex-KENT) and the JOHN L. CLEM (ex-IRWIN), sister ships built by William Cramp and Sons in 1918. Almost as old (built 1920) were the two Hog Islanders in the list, namely the CHATEAU THIERRY and the ST. MIHIEL, veterans of the Army Transport Service. Also built in 1920 were the WILLIAM L. THOMPSON and the PRESIDENT FILLMORE. The MUNARGO (1921), the MANUEL ARNUS (1923) and the ALGONQUIN (1926) completed the ten vessels originally considered for use as Army hospital ships. Altogether it was a job lot of older craft, none of which at the most had a speed of more than 14 to 15 knots, and all of which had seen better days.[40]

Of the above-mentioned ten ships, the MANUEL ARNUS, a damaged vessel of Mexican registry, subsequently was returned to the War Shipping Administration because she proved too expensive to convert. Also, nothing came of the plans to convert the WILLIAM L. THOMPSON. Actually, in June 1943 the AGWILEON was the only vessel available for conversion, which was accomplished at New York. Renamed the SHAMROCK in August 1943, this vessel was the third Army hospital ship to be placed in operation in that

---

[40] Originally Mr. George A. Anthony, Maintenance and Repair Branch, Water Division, OCT, had included among 13 Army transports suitable for conversion the SHAWNEE, EVANGELINE, SIBONEY, MONTEREY, and MEXICO, which he "considered decidedly superior for hospital use to such vessels as the CHATEAU THIERRY, ST. MIHIEL, THOMPSON, CLEM, and HINDS." See his Memorandum of 1 June 1943 for Lt. Col. O. Y. Warren.

U. S. ARMY HOSPITAL SHIP LARKSPUR

Built in 1901, this vessel served in both the Imperial
German Navy and the United States Navy prior to conversion into a United States Army hospital ship

U S ARMY HOSPITAL SHIP
L A R K S P U R

year.

The remaining vessels of the original ten could not be touched until replacements were ready. In fact, late in June 1943, three of the vessels involved, namely the MUNARGO (AP 20), the CHATEAU THIERRY (AP 31), and the ST. MIHIEL (AP 32) were still in the service of the Navy Department which had agreed to return them to the War Department but had stipulated that the dates of reversion to the Army were "contingent upon their being replaced by Army allocated cargo vessels to be converted to carry troops in 'tween deck spaces."

Although the general objectives remained unchanged, completion of the Army hospital ship program in 1943 was in a state of uncertainty. Various vessels were considered but could not be included, either because they were unsuitable for the purpose, or because they could not be spared from current assignments. But in the fall of 1943 a decision was finally reached to convert six Liberty ships into hospital craft. The vessels nominated were the GEORGE WASHINGTON CARVER, the SAMUEL F. B. MORSE, the ST. OLAF, the STANFORD WHITE, the WILLIAM OSLER, and the ZEBULON B. VANCE. Thus at length the original objections to the employment of the EC2 type were overcome, and after conversion and change of name of all except the ST. OLAF, these six vessels ultimately became Army hospital ships.

Aside from the above-noted Liberty ships, which were originally turned out in 1942-43 as cargo carriers, the remaining additions to the Army hospital fleet in 1944 consisted of older passenger vessels such as the BRIDGEPORT (ex-BRESLAU), a German-built vessel dating from 1901; the SIBONEY, a veteran of the first World War; and the PRESIDENT BUCHANAN, constructed in 1920. Under the stress of global warfare available shipping had become so scarce that, in general, only old and comparatively slow vessels could be spared for conversion into Army hospital ships. Thus, the BRIDGEPORT when acquired by the Army in September 1943, was forty-two years old and had a speed of only ten knots.

As of October 1944 only two of the original twenty-four hospital ships planned for Army use remain to be completed, presumably early in 1945. These two vessels are the ERNESTINE KORANDA (ex-DOROTHY LUCKENBACH) and the LOUIS A. MILNE (ex-LEWIS LUCKENBACH). When completed, the 24 vessels in the hospital fleet were to have a total patient capacity of more than 14,000.

Role of the Chief of Transportation and the Surgeon General

From the outset the Chief of Transportation, Major General Gross, together with Brig. Gen. R. H. Wylie, took an active interest in the Army hospital ship program. As early as March 1942 General (then Colonel) C. P. Gross had insisted that the Army should have its own hospital ships, in contradistinction to the viewpoint of Admiral Land that such vessels fell properly under the cognizance of the Navy Department. General Wylie personally participated in the important conference of 12 April 1943 at which representatives of the Chief of Transportation, the Surgeon General, and the Planning Division, Army Service Forces, laid the groundwork for a fleet of convention-protected Army hospital ships.

In the Office of the Chief of Transportation the Army hospital ship program became the special responsibility of the Water Division at

Washington and the respective Army ports of embarkation which supervised the actual conversions. Within the Water Division the Maintenance and Repair Branch occupied a key position from a technical standpoint in the accomplishment of conversions to Army hospital ships, reporting periodically to the Chief of the Division on the progress made. As already noted, the Ship Operations Branch arranged for the formal designation of each hospital ship and exercised certain administrative and technical supervision after the vessel was placed in operation. In April 1944, in conjunction with the Movements Division, OCT, a new Aircraft and Troop Transport Branch in the Water Division was assigned the task of scheduling the movements of Army hospital ships. Finally, mention must be made of the Ship Conversion Unit, established at New York in January 1944, which, among other things, was charged with supervision of the drawing of all plans and layouts for hospital ships. However, the actual day-to-day problems relating to the various hospital ship conversions fell most heavily upon the ports to which such jobs had been assigned. Thus, New York was responsible for the first Army hospital ship, the ACADIA; New Orleans supervised the conversion of the ALGONQUIN; Boston had the ST. OLAF; San Francisco the ERNEST HINDS, and Seattle the MARIGOLD. In a sense, each conversion was a special problem calling for cooperative effort by the Transportation Corps both at Washington and in the field.

Important also was the role of the Surgeon General. Since 1941 the Office of the Surgeon General had been alert to the need of Army hospital ships and had participated actively in the planning to that end. Acting through a technical staff in Washington and the port surgeons at the Army ports of embarkation, the Surgeon General supervised, from the medical standpoint, conversion of the hospital ships. He determined the necessary medical equipment, facilities, and supplies, and when the vessel was ready for service, he also provided the required medical personnel. The ACADIA, for instance, in addition to an authorized civilian operating crew (Transportation Corps) of 164, carried military personnel numbering 160, including doctors, nurses and medical corpsmen. On occasion, the Surgeon General rejected certain vessels, notably the old UTAHAN, as unsuitable for conversion into hospital ships, and at all times his representatives kept a watchful eye on the alterations being made on each vessel. In general, it can be said that conversions of hospital ships have been made to conform so far as is practicable and possible to the requirements of the Surgeon General.

Thanks to the efforts of the Surgeon General and of the Chief of Transportation each ship when completed was essentially a floating hospital. The ALGONQUIN, for example, has a complete operating room, pharmacy, dental laboratory, autopsy room and morgue, an X-ray room, diet kitchens, wards for various types of patients, and even a laundry, all fitted with most modern equipment. This vessel can accommodate 460 bed patients. Conversion of the ALGONQUIN was begun 19 July 1943 and completed 25 January 1944 at Mobile under the supervision of the Port Surgeon at New Orleans. The total cost of the vessel was approximately $2,000,000.

V

THE NAMING OF ARMY HOSPITAL SHIPS

There was no established policy in 1943 to cover the assignment of names to Army hospital ships. In the past such craft generally had retained the original name while in the service of the Army, with the exception of the Army hospital ship RELIEF (ex-JOHN ENGLIS), which was operated during the War with Spain. During World War I the Army had no hospital ship under its jurisdiction, and as a result had no occasion to develop any precedent for the naming of a vessel of this character.

Temporary Expedients

When the ACADIA and the SEMINOLE began their careers as Army hospital ships in the summer of 1943, there was no change in name. Nor was there any apparent need thereof, since both vessels were well known, and a new name might simply confuse the enemy and serve no useful purpose. But as additional vessels were selected for conversion which carried names that, if not objectionable per se, nevertheless were hardly suitable for hospital ships, it appeared advisable to adopt some definite naming policy.

Use of Names of Flowers

On 1 July 1943 the Office of the Surgeon General (Col. John A. Rogers) submitted the following recommendation to the Adjutant General:

> "The War Department has authorized the conversion of a certain number of ships to be used as hospital ships under control of the Army. These ships will be operated under the provisions of the Geneva Convention, that is, will sail unarmed, are specially painted, and will utilize all lights at night,

It is deemed highly desirable that each be given a name
which will tend to identify them as hospital ships. In
order not to trespass on the series of names given to
various types of naval vessels, it is recommended that
Army hospital ships be named for flowers. Flowers indi-
cate a quality of mercy and from many are obtained cura-
tive drugs used in the treatment of the sick."

As appropriate names Colonel Rogers next listed alphabetically

twenty-four flowers, beginning with arbutus and ending with zinnia,

which he suggested be used for "all ships converted to hospital ships

in the future." The recommendation was not without merit. The list,

however, included a number of flowers not widely known in the United

States, such as the yucca. Others like the Forsythia and the rhododen-

dron were hardly more than flowering shrubs. Still others, it may be

noted, were scarcely American flowers: this, for instance, was true

of the edelweiss, a small perennial herb that grows high in the Alps.

In due course the above recommendation by Colonel Rogers reached

the Office of the Chief of Transportation, where after preliminary con-

sideration by the Ship Operations Branch, Water Division, the following

memorandum was forwarded on 22 July 1943 to the Surgeon General by Col.

Clifford Starr, Chief, Administrative Division:

"1.   Reference is made to your memorandum of July 1,
addressed to The Adjutant General, and transmitted to the Chief
of Transportation as a matter pertaining to that office.

"2.   Under applicable treaties, hospital ships will be
registered by name, and notice of assignment of the particular ship as a hospital ship will, through proper channels, be
given to enemy governments.

"3.   All these ships now appear in the shipping regis-
ters throughout the world, identified by their present names
plus the physical characteristics of the respective vessels. It
may well be assumed that the physical characteristics and the

silhouette of the vessel, associated with the present name
of the vessel, are well-known to the enemy. Notwithstand-
ing the fact that hospital ships will at all times display
specified distinguishing marks, physical characteristics
and silhouette as factors for ready identification, are important.

"4.   This office concurs in the idea of names of
flowers for hospital ships. However, in the interest of the
use of every caution, for the reasons set out above, it has
been the view of this office that changes in the names of
vessels to be converted to hospital ships should be confined
to those whose present names are entirely inconsistent with
the idea of a name for a hospital ship.

"5.   Of the ten vessels presently scheduled for conversion to hospital ships, five now have names considered
repugnant to the idea of the name of a hospital ship; and
for these, this office will be pleased to undertake the
assignment of names from the list of names recommended by
your office. Having in mind that the names selected should
be appropriate at once for a ship and a hospital, it is proposed that the new names to be assigned to hospital ships be
selected from the following recommended by your office.

Jasmine	Poppy	Wisteria
Kalmia	Shamrock	Yucca
Larkspur	Thistle	Zinnia "
Marigold		

Also on 22 July 1943 the Chief of the Water Division, Col. R. M.

Hicks, proposed to the Chief of Transportation that the names Shamrock,

Larkspur, Marigold, Wisteria and Thistle be used for the next five hos-

pital ships. In accordance with this proposal the old AGWILEON was to

be renamed the SHAMROCK.[41] On 27 July 1943, since it had title to these

vessels, approval of the War Shipping Administration was requested by

Col. Hicks for changing the names of the AGWILEON, of the MANUEL ARNUS,

---

[41]
By Circular No. 102, OCT, 13 August 1943, "the SS AGWILEON operated
as United States Army transport, on bareboat basis," was assigned
the name SHAMROCK.

- 43 -

and of the PRESIDENT FILLMORE. The latter two were to be called, respectively, the LARKSPUR and the MARIGOLD, but later when the MANUEL ARNUS was dropped from consideration as a hospital ship, the name LARKSPUR was transferred to the old BRIDGEPORT.

The matter of establishing names for the Army hospital ships was more important than might appear, since each vessel had to be registered officially as to name and characteristics so as to be readily recognizable by the enemy. Once a name had been so registered, any change had to be communicated to the enemy through the State Department and the Swiss Government. Moreover, as previously noted, there were several instances in which the vessel was so well known in the shipping world as to make renaming inadvisable. Thus, a number of hospital ships continued to serve under their old names, among which may be mentioned the ACADIA, the ALGONQUIN, the CHATEAU THIERRY, the ST. MIHIEL and the SEMINOLE.

The Coast Guard Objects

Throughout 1943 and the early part of 1944 the Secretary of War continued to inform the Secretary of State that certain vessels under conversion had been designated to serve as Army hospital ships. Included among these ships were several bearing the names of flowers that had been approved by the Office of the Surgeon General and the Office of the Chief of Transportation. On 5 February 1944 the Chief of Transportation extended the use of flowers to provide new names for the six Liberty ships that had been selected for conversion in the fall of 1943.[42]

---

[42] TC Circular No. 80-4, 5 February 1944. The circular also formally assigned the new name LARKSPUR to the BRIDGEPORT.

U. S. ARMY HOSPITAL SHIP ST. OLAF

A former Liberty ship, the ST. OLAF illustrates this

type of conversion

Thus the WILLIAM OSLER, honoring the distinguished Canadian-born physician and former professor at the Johns Hopkins University, Sir William Osler, was renamed the WISTERIA; and the ST. OLAF, named after the Norwegian patron saint, was to be known henceforth as the JASMINE. At the time the choice of these names went apparently unchallenged, since it was, to be sure, in accordance with the prevailing policy.

In March 1944 the policy of adopting the names of flowers was questioned. Under date of 3 March the Commandant of the United States Coast Guard, Rear Admiral R. R. Waesche sent the following communication to the Chief of Transportation, Major General C. P. Gross:

> "It is noted by a dispatch from the Commander in Chief, United States Fleet, under date of 29 February 1944, that in naming new War Department hospital ships four are given the names of JASMINE, MARIGOLD, DOGWOOD and WISTERIA, which are the same as Coast Guard Cutters in active service for many years.
>
> "In naming Navy and Coast Guard vessels, the established policy has been to avoid the selection of names which already designate ships in active service. It has been found in following this procedure that confusion has been avoided in administrative matters, communications and especially in mail delivery etc.
>
> "Do you concur that it is desirable to arrange for similar checking to avoid name duplication of Army and Coast Guard vessels? If so will you kindly designate the War Department representative whom the Coast Guard Office of Operations may contact to arrange details."

On 9 March 1944 General Gross sent the following reply to Admiral Waesche:

> "This will acknowledge receipt of your letter of 3 March 1944 (CG-601) in regard to selection of the names of JASMINE, MARIGOLD, DOGWOOD and WISTERIA for War Department hospital ships, which names had been assigned to Coast Guard Cutters.

"In accordance with an agreement reached with Rear Admiral Charles A. Park of your office, the names which have been assigned to the following hospital ships, and registered through the State Department with foreign governments in accordance with the Geneva Conference, will remain as designated:

JASMINE	WISTERIA	SHAMROCK
MARIGOLD	THISTLE	LARKSPUR
DOGWOOD		

"In the future, before assigning the names of flowers to War Department hospital ships and registering them with foreign governments in accordance with the Geneva Conference, your office will be contacted by the Chief of Water Division, Transportation Corps, in order to avoid duplication of names."

The ST. OLAF

In his letter of 9 March 1944 to Admiral Waesche General Gross stated that the Army hospital ship JASMINE would remain as designated.[43] This vessel which had a proposed patient capacity of 627 was then being converted at Boston and was due to be completed on 10 June 1944. Although full details are not presently available, it was evidently felt in certain quarters, notably in the State Department and in the War Shipping Administration, that the original name ST. OLAF, the patron saint of Norway, should have been retained out of respect for a fighting ally among the United Nations. Accordingly on 25 March 1944 the vessel was redesignated the ST. OLAF.[44]

Present Policy

Following the objection raised by Admiral Waesche and the incident

---

[43] Notification of the new name had already been forwarded to the enemy in the usual manner.

[44] TC Circular No. 80-4, Supplement No. 2, 25 March 1944.

of the ST. OLAF, no more hospital ships were named after flowers. As
a result, only six vessels remained in this category, specifically,
the DOGWOOD, LARKSPUR, MARIGOLD, SHAMROCK, THISTLE, and WISTERIA. On
10 March 1944 in a memorandum for the Chief of Transportation, Brig.
Gen. R. W. Bliss of the Surgeon General's Office recommended a new naming policy. Since flowers were banned, he suggested that the remaining
hospital ships be named as follows: six after famous doctors, six after
famous nurses, and six after medical schools. It proved difficult to
decide among the various medical schools,[45] and this part of the plan
therefore was soon dropped.

The upshot of deliberation on the matter by the Office of the Surgeon General was the decision reached in March 1944 to recommend naming
the rest of the Army hospital ships after deceased Army doctors and Army
nurses who had served with distinction.[46] The first person so honored
was the late Emily H. M. Weder, a regular Army nurse since 1918, who
died in February 1944 at the Walter Reed General Hospital, Washington,
D. C. In contradistinction to the frequent practice of honoring parti-
cipants in past conflicts, the Office of the Surgeon General has selected
the names of persons who have played heroic roles in the present war.
Among such Army doctors and Army nurses whose names have been assigned
to hospital ships may be mentioned First Lieutenant Blanche F. Sigman,

---

[45] Among others were suggested the medical schools at Tufts College, at
Tulane and at Northwestern University.

[46] The Ship Operations Branch, Water Division, continued to arrange for
the naming and designating of Army hospital ships.

who was killed in action on the Anzio beachhead; Colonel Jarrett M. Huddleston, also killed in Italy; Major John J. Meany, slain in the North African Theater; and Captain Charles A. Stafford who was killed during the evacuation of Java. As already noted, at present (October 1944) two hospital ships are still under conversion. The one, the ERNESTINE KORANDA, was named after an Army nurse; the other, the LOUIS A. MILNE, honors the late Port Surgeon at New York.

VI

ADMINISTRATION AND OPERATION OF THE
ARMY HOSPITAL SHIPS

Including the Navy-owned and operated vessels, the COMFORT, HOPE and MERCY, the Army ultimately will have in its service a fleet of 24 hospital ships with a total patient capacity of 14,531. The administration and operation of these vessels require close cooperation of both the Army and the Navy. Within the War Department the Chief of Transportation and the Surgeon General are directly responsible for the Army hospital ships. The former operates the 21 Army-owned (or bareboated) vessels, and the latter provides the medical staff for the entire fleet including the three ships owned and operated by the Navy. The overseas commanders arrange for assembling the sick and wounded to be evacuated from their respective theaters of operation. Altogether, the movement of such passengers by Army hospital ship to the United States is a complex process distinctly different from the usual overseas troop movement.

Requirements of the Hague Convention X of 1907

The Hague Convention X of 1907 represents the adaptation to maritime warfare of the principles of the Geneva Convention. In compliance therewith Army hospital ships are subject to certain specific requirements.[47] First, their mission must be clearly indicated. The hull and superstructure must be painted white and the vessel must carry the pre-

_____

[47] See AR 55-530, 30 December 1943.

scribed markings such as the horizontal green band on both sides and the familiar red crosses on sides, deck, and funnel, so as to be recognizable instantly as a hospital ship. Lifeboats and life rafts must be similarly painted and marked. Each vessel travels unarmed, and is required to "fly with the United States flag, a white flag with a red cross." In contrast to the customary wartime practice of concealing completely the identity of the vessel, the name of each Army hospital ship stands out boldly on the port and starboard sides of the bow and on the center line of the stern. Before being actually employed as a hospital ship the name and physical characteristics of the vessel are communicated to the enemy. At night the mission of the vessel is made clear by continuous illumination from sunset to sunrise.[48]

Aside from the prescribed painting and marking, each hospital ship must be operated strictly in accordance with international practice. In addition to patients, each vessel has only the necessary operating crew and the required medical personnel, since the presence of other persons might compromise the protected status of the ship. The operating personnel carry identification cards and are provided with Red Cross brassards.[49] Only certain prescribed documents are permitted aboard the vessel.[50] Radio silence is observed except in an extreme emergency. Hospital ships may

---

[48] "Except in cases where emergency requires that the ship be darkened." See AR 55-530, CI, 4 May 1944.

[49] See War Department Circular No. 343, 30 December 1943, par. 11, d (3); and No. 230, 13 July 1942, par. 1.

[50] See War Department Circular No. 374, 14 September 1944, sec. II.

not be used for any military purposes, and they may be intercepted, searched or even detained by the enemy. An enemy warship may even demand the surrender of the sick, wounded or shipwrecked men on board the hospital ship.[51]

Operating Personnel on Army Hospital Ships

The operating personnel on Army hospital ships consists of the crew (civilian) and the medical complement (military). The master has jurisdiction over the civilian crew, all of whom are employed by the Transportation Corps under civil service regulations and in accordance with the authorized crew strength for each vessel. The master is in supreme command of the ship and of all persons on board who sign the ship's articles. He is responsible for and has full control of (1) the technical operation, navigation, and safety of the ship as required by the navigation laws and rules of the United States; (2) the safe delivery of passengers and cargo at destination; (3) the discipline and efficiency of the crew, except enlisted men permanently attached to the ship.[52] At present (1944) the Army hospital ships carry full civilian crews although at one time it was contemplated that enlisted men might be used

---

[51] Cf. the first "tentative instructions" for hospital ships, which were sent by the Movements Division to the Commanding General, New York Port of Embarkation, on 4 June 1943. These consisted largely of abstracts from the applicable provisions of the Hague Convention X of 1907. The occasion was the initial voyage of the ACADIA as a convention-protected hospital ship.

[52] AR 55-325, 5 November 1942.

for the Steward's Department.[53]

The senior medical officer aboard a hospital ship is designated as the hospital ship commander but is also the ship surgeon, thus serving in a dual capacity. As hospital ship commander he reports through the usual channels of command to the commander at the home port of the vessel, performing the duties, insofar as applicable, that are prescribed for an Army transport commander. As ship's surgeon he has the duties assigned to a transport surgeon, and while acting in this capacity he is under the technical supervision of the port surgeon at the home port of the vessel. These two functions are separate.

Basically, however, the hospital ship commander is responsible for the administrative and technical supervision of the medical complement and for the medical care given to all patients on board.[54] Analysis of the composition of the medical staff aboard the ACADIA will serve to illustrate the general division of functions among the military personnel under the supervision of the hospital ship commander. As of June 1944 the 204th Hospital Complement assigned to this vessel included, among others, 14 medical and dental officers, 37 Army nurses, a dietitian, two physiotherapists, two chaplains, an American Red Cross worker, and 146

---

[53] The Superintendent of the Water Division at the New York Port of Embarkation questioned the wisdom of this arrangement, and subsequently, with the concurrence of the Office of the Surgeon General, the Chief of the Water Division decided to employ "a full civilian crew" in the interest of "more efficient operation" and in order to "preclude any possible labor difficulty arising from the use of combined military and civilian crews." Memorandum of 23 February 1944 from Chief, Water Division, to Ship Conversion Unit, TC.

[54] Cf. TC Circular No. 80-14, revised, dated 15 May 1944.

enlisted men (including four radio operators). The major portion of the military personnel consisted of Army nurses and medical corpsmen.

Operating Problems

At the outset one of the chief operating problems of the Army hospital ship appears to have involved defining the respective responsibilities and duties of the civilian and the military personnel with regard to the preparation and serving of meals, room service, laundry service, and the policing of the vessel. On 10 December 1943 the Chief of Transportation issued detailed instructions concerning these matters, which with some revision were distributed again on 15 March and on 15 May 1944. Briefly, as last issued, these instructions make the civilian crew responsible for the preparation of food for all persons on board the ship, except for supplementary dietary items which are prepared by the military crew. The civilian crew provides its own dining room and messroom service and its own room service. It also polices the spaces used by the civilian ship's officers and crew.[55]

The military crew, on the other hand, provides messroom service for all military enlisted crew; dining room and tray service for all patients and/or casuals; room service for the entire military crew and for all patients and/or casuals. The military crew polices all areas such as bathrooms and diet kitchens used exclusively by military personnel. It is responsible for the washing of the chinaware, glassware,

---

[55] In addition, the civilian crew provides "dining room service to military personnel assigned to duty aboard the vessel and authorized subsistence in the saloon mess."

silverware, and trays used in serving meals to permanent military enlisted personnel, patients, and/or casuals. It also operates the laundry when such facilities are available.[56] Finally, it provides guards
for designated sections of the vessel.

Apart from the establishment of the above-noted division of labor
among the civilian and military personnel, the operating problems of
Army hospital ships apparently have been much as one might expect on
vessels of this character. Despite the fact that the civilian crew members are paid on a full wartime basis and are relatively safer from enemy action than when employed on a troop transport, the manning of the
hospital ships has proved no easy assignment. Although the crew members
are encouraged to stay with their ships, there is a considerable turn-
over in the operating departments. The proper care of the patients on
board is a continuing problem calling for the utmost vigilance on the
part of the medical staff. The providing of adequate ventilation has
often proved difficult. Supplying the food alone for a single voyage
poses a problem in these days of rationing and shortages.

The problem of maintaining an adequate supply of fresh water
while at sea has become far less serious than formerly as a result
of the development by the Office of the Surgeon General of a new
process whereby laundry can be washed in sea water. By means of
sea-water laundering enroute, it is estimated that a saving of approximately two-thirds of the linen inventory can be effected, thus releasing

---

[56] Laundry facilities aboard hospital ships "are to be utilized primar-
ily for hospital and ship's laundry." Such laundry consists chiefly
of linen and bedding; for further details as to laundry operations
see TC Circular 80-14, revised, 15 May 1944, par. II.

additional space for returning patients.[57] Finally, Army hospital
ships have required more than the usual maintenance and repair, since
the aim is not only to keep them in the best operating condition but
also to make them as attractive as possible. The Chief of the Water
Division at Washington, D. C., Col. R. M. Hicks, has set a high standard for these vessels. "Their mission," he says, "demands that they
be the best and most efficient ships operated by the Transportation
Corps."[58]

Charleston as the Home Port of the Army Hospital Ships

Both the ACADIA and the SEMINOLE sailed from New York on their
maiden voyages as convention-protected Army hospital ships. But as
the principal Army port of embarkation on the Atlantic seaboard, New
York was already too heavily burdened with troop and cargo movements
to justify its use as the home port of the Army hospital ships. In
the meantime, during the fall of 1942 while the ACADIA was still being
converted at Boston into a combination trooper and ambulance ship, plans
were being laid to utilize Charleston as the home port of at least one
Army hospital ship.

By memorandum of 25 September 1942 to the Chief of Transportation
at Washington, D. C., Col. H. J. Farner, Executive Officer at the
Charleston Port of Embarkation, called attention to the need of an Army
hospital ship for this installation. At this time each port was charged

---

[57] See release of 15 September 1944, Bureau of Public Relations, War
Department. A hospital ship uses literally thousands of sheets.

[58] See his remarks at the Meeting of Superintendents of Water Divisions
at Chicago, Illinois, on 7 July 1944.

with the evacuation of sick and wounded from the respective overseas forces which it supplied; and in the absence of Army hospital ships, evacuation in general was accomplished by the use of hospital spaces on returning troop transports. This plan presented no difficulties in the larger ports where troop ships operated on a regular schedule. But as Col. Farner noted, only supply ships docked regularly at Charleston. Furthermore, the bases served by this port were "located in an area...noteworthy for rare and deadly diseases and parasites," and the estimated number of evacuees therefrom was, he said, more than enough to justify the request for a hospital ship of 500 patient capacity. According to Col. Farner, "the close proximity of Army General Hospitals, the excellence of rail transportation and the geographic location" served to make the Charleston Port of Embarkation "ideal for overseas evacuation."[59]

For the time being nothing came of Col. Farner's request for a hospital ship at Charleston. But the facilities at that port were not overlooked, and in compliance with instructions of 27 October 1942 from the Chief of Transportation evacuation plans were made by the Port Surgeon on 9 November 1942 to cover all sick and wounded expected on the basis of the troop strength of the overseas areas then being supplied from Charleston, namely Bermuda, Ascension Island, India and China. In addition, on 19 November 1942 the Port Surgeon prepared detailed overseas evacuation plans designed to care for emergency shipments of casualties

---

[59] To these advantages Col. Farner might also have added the mild climate of Charleston, facilitating debarkation in all months of the year.

from the North African campaign. These plans comprehended both expected and unexpected debarkations of patients. Litter and mental cases were to be placed in Stark General Hospital but arrangements were made to utilize other Army hospitals in the South, so as to assure, if necessary, a total of 14,200 beds.

The above planning proved of great value when approximately one year later, on 1 November 1943, the first three Army hospital ships were assigned to the Charleston Port of Embarkation. These were the ACADIA, the SEMINOLE, and the SHAMROCK. After months of hard service overseas evacuating casualties from North Africa to the United Kingdom, the ACADIA arrived at Charleston on 5 November 1943 with a full load of casualties, the first of the Army hospital ships to reach the new port. Subsequently, as additional Army hospital ships were placed in service, all were assigned to the Charleston Port of Embarkation. So far as is known no directive was issued designating Charleston as the home port of the Army hospital fleet.[60] In fact, its function as such was long concealed in the press under the familiar World War I guise of "An East Coast Port."[61]

The handling of the Army hospital ships at Charleston has developed into a major activity of the port. Each of these ships must be manned, supplied, maintained and repaired. Since all the vessels are converted craft which are frequently overseas for months at a time, they are in-

---

[60] The Army hospital ships operating from Charleston served the North African and European theaters. Evacuations from the Pacific were handled by the Navy.

[61] The secrecy was more apparent than real. Cf. the New York Times story published 10 January 1944, which tells of patients being taken from the ACADIA to Stark General Hospital.

variably in need of repairs, supplies, or equipment upon the return to the home port. Depending upon the size, the unloading of a single hospital ship may require from three to five hours, and trained and efficient personnel are necessary. Litters, litter bearers and special vehicles must all be provided.

In order to facilitate the plans for receiving and moving patients from overseas, within 24 hours after the departure of the hospital ship from the overseas port the commander of the home port is advised by radio as to the anticipated time of arrival and the number of patients by class. This information is of value only as a guide, since storms or mechanical difficulties may delay the ship. A boarding party, headed by the Superintendent of the Water Division, meets the vessel upon arrival in Charleston harbor. While the ship is docking, the Port Surgeon confers with the Hospital Ship Commander and conducts an inspection of the ship and the medical personnel. Each evacuee is also marked with a tag indicating the ward to which he will be moved. In addition each patient carries a debarkation tag fastened to his outer clothing, which gives his name, rank, serial number, class, and a brief diagnosis.[62] This tag is prepared by the personnel of the Hospital Ship Complement during the voyage, and the lower portion of it is perforated in such a way that a stub may be torn off to serve as a receipt for each patient

---

[62] On 19 July 1944, in order to protect mental and venereal patients from "slighting remarks and crude humor from fellow patients or others," the Chief of Transportation directed that this tag henceforth should contain "only a letter indicating the medical classification of the patient." See TC Circular No. 50-31, revised, 17 July 1944.

DEBARKATION SCENE AT CHARLESTON

Litters are in place and medical corpsmen stand
ready to evacuate the sick and wounded arriving
at the port

debarked.

In the interest of the safety of the patients, evacuation of the hospital ship takes place only during the daylight hours. The Port Surgeon must estimate the number of personnel needed in the various categories such as medical officers, mental attendants, litter bearers and ambulance drivers, all depending upon the number of patients to be evacuated. Motor transportation requirements must be estimated. Sufficient space must be allowed for personal effects carried by patients as well as for patients in casts and on crutches. Litter patients and mental patients of the violent type are transported in ambulances. Ambulant and troop class patients are moved by bus.[63]

During November 1943, the first month in which the Army hospital ships docked at Charleston, some 1,128 Army patients were debarked. Subsequently, during the winter and spring months of 1943-44 the port was concerned chiefly with evacuees from North Africa. The peak of the North African movement was reached during May 1944 with a total of 2,581 patients. The Normandy landings in the following month were reflected by a total of 460 patients evacuated from the United Kingdom. All patients received in August 1944 were from that same area. Thanks to additional vessels in operation the total number of patients evacuated at Charleston in September 1944 reached a new high of 4,273, of whom 1,652 were from the United Kingdom and 2,621 were from North Africa. The figures here cited by no means tell the complete story of the activity

---

[63] For further details see the account prepared by Major Sidney Robbin and Captain T. G. Scott for the H̲i̲s̲t̲o̲r̲i̲c̲a̲l̲ ̲R̲e̲c̲o̲r̲d̲, Charleston Port of Embarkation, 1944.

of the Army hospital ships, since many of the vessels have remained overseas for months at a time engaged in local operations between Mediterranean ports such as Naples and Oran.

Life Aboard an Army Hospital Ship

Life on the average Army hospital ship is by no means grim, despite the inevitable pain and suffering among the patients. The Chief of Transportation and the Surgeon General have spared no effort in order to make the voyage to the United States as comfortable and pleasant as is humanly possible. To this end each patient receives the best possible treatment from highly trained personnel operating with the most modern equipment available. Excellent food, comfortable beds, "movies," musical recordings and other recreational features make up the prescription to bolster the morale and to hasten the recovery of the war-worn veterans.

On every hospital ship food is an important item.[64] The quantities involved are staggering. A single hospital ship may carry more than 8,000 quarts of frozen homogenized milk and 9,000 strictly fresh eggs. In addition to the regular menus, special diets must be prepared in the diet kitchens for certain types of patients such as those suffering from gastric ulcer, diabetes, or jaundice. Working closely with the Chief Steward, the dietitian supervises the preparation and service of the food for all patients on board. By means of an elaborate food

---

[64] Cf. the unsigned article "Food Problems on a Hospital Ship," published in the Army Day Review (Washington, D. C.), 6 April 1944, p. 236.

MEDICAL WARD, A DECK, U. S. ARMY

HOSPITAL SHIP EMILY H. M. WEDER

War-weary veterans rest on comfortable mattresses

aboard this Army hospital ship

storage system meats, fruits and vegetables can be kept fresh for approximately ninety days.

For breakfast, weekday menus contain such familiar offerings as hominy grits, bacon, eggs, and coffee; and, for luncheon and dinner, boiled ham, potatoes, beans, bread and butter, apple pie, cheese and coffee. Frozen milk and ice cream rate high with most patients. On Sundays and holidays the menus are more elaborate than usual. On the ACADIA, for example, the Christmas Day dinner at sea (1943) matched that served by many a swank New York restaurant. On the menu for that day traditional American foods like roast Vermont turkey and hot mince pie were surrounded by the usual French flourishes of the Chef de Cuisine (Monsieur Luis Orbe), whereby a stalk of celery appeared as celery en branche and buttered asparagus became asparagus au beurre.

Much of the therapeutic value of the homeward passage lies in the abrupt change from front-line hardship to the comparative luxury of the Army hospital ship. Clean beds, good food, the quiet comfort of an ocean voyage where every need is met, all this must be heaven to the returning soldier after long months in combat. Once the patient is on board his spirits are never allowed to flag. A public address system carries the latest song hits through loudspeakers into every ward. All ships have musical instruments on hand, and on practically every voyage the ambulant patients stage their own amateur hour. The MARIGOLD boasts her own volunteer band with a crooner and with its own arrangements of everything from "boogie-woogie" to the ranking favorite overseas, the story of "Lili Marlene."[65] A ship's newspaper helps keep the patients both informed and entertained.[66] The ACADIA, for example, publishes the Fore and Aft, the LARKSPUR, the News Buoy, and the WISTERIA, the Salt Shaker. Issued in mimeographed form, such publications contain the latest news briefs, poems and stories contributed by patients, Army cartoons, and informational material on the hospital facilities at Charleston.[67] A Red Cross worker circulating through the wards lends a kindly hand, gives instruction in handicraft, and supplies reading matter from the ship's library. The Red Cross representative also provides recreational material, hometown newspapers and musical instruments, together with such necessities as combs, toothbrushes, shaving cream, and razor blades. Games, quiz programs, and similar entertainment serve to while away the hours at sea. The religious element is not forgotten. Protestant and Catholic Chaplains minister to the members of their respective faiths and act as special service officers.

---

[65] See the release of 24 October 1944, War Department, Bureau of Public Relations, on "jive" as a boon to patients aboard U. S. hospital ships.

[66] These news sheets were developed and promoted through the efforts of the Assistant Special Service Officer at Charleston, 2nd Lt. Robert A. Schiller.

[67] Cf. the release of 19 May 1944, War Department, Bureau of Public Relations. See G. I. Galley, vol. 1, no. 28 (New York, N.Y.), November 1944, pp. 2-3.

VII

THE CURRENT SITUATION

Until late in 1944 all the Army hospital ships were assigned to the Charleston Port of Embarkation and all were engaged exclusively in evacuating casualties from the North African and European theaters. Meanwhile the three Navy-owned and operated hospital ships in the service of the Army, namely the COMFORT, HOPE, and MERCY, were based at the Los Angeles Port of Embarkation, to which they evacuated casualties from the Pacific area.[68]

The Problem of the Pacific

Of necessity the initial evacuation in 1942 of Army patients in the Pacific was accomplished by the use of returning transports and the regular Navy hospital ships. No conversion work was done on the COMFORT, HOPE, and MERCY until 1943 and by January 1944 it became apparent that additional hospital ship space would be required for the Pacific. By letter of 29 January 1944 the Chief of Transportation informed the Commanding Generals of the Central, South, and Southwest Pacific Areas of the details of the Army hospital ship program; listed five additional Army hospital ships to be assigned to the Pacific, to-

---

[68] On these vessels the Army provides the required medical staff and attention for the patients on board. The respective responsibilities of personnel of the Army and the Navy on these ships were determined by agreement between the Chief of Transportation, Major General C. P. Gross, and the Director, Naval Transportation Service, Rear Admiral W. W. Smith. See Memorandum of 22 August 1944, Major General Gross to Admiral Smith.

gether with certain proposed itineraries; and, lastly, requested general comments from the theaters.[69]

Under date of 23 February 1944 the Office of the Commanding General, Central Pacific Area, reported to the Chief of Transportation at Washington, D. C., that one hospital ship (about 600 patient capacity) would be required to evacuate patients regularly at 30 day intervals from Honolulu to the mainland. Several more hospital ships, it was noted, would be needed for future operations. Although the request was repeated, considerable time was required before any action could be taken, and the Commanding General, Central Pacific Area, was so advised by radiogram of 9 May 1944 from Lt. Col. D. E. Farr, Chief, Overseas Troop Branch, Movements Division. Because of delay in the conversion program and the need of hospital ships in the Atlantic, Lt. Col. Farr thought it would not be possible to provide the Central Pacific Area with a hospital ship until August 1944.

Late in the fall of 1944, as the landing of General MacArthur's forces at Leyte in the Philippines heralded new advances in the Pacific, two Army hospital ships were transferred from the Charleston to the Los Angeles Port of Embarkation.[70] This action foreshadowed the ultimate deployment of additional Army hospital ships to the Pacific as the need arose.

---

69   The Deputy Commander of the South Pacific Area reported on 11 February 1944 that it was impossible to forecast, with sufficient accuracy, local needs for hospital ships. No report appears to have been received from the Southwest Pacific.

70   The MARIGOLD was transferred on 16 October 1944 and the EMILY H. M. WEDER was scheduled for transfer approximately 1 November 1944.

Present Procedure

A uniform procedure for evacuation of patients by water or air from overseas commands to the United States was prescribed in a long detailed letter of 8 June 1944 issued by the Adjutant General.[71] According to this letter, the so-called "helpless fraction" of patients would be evacuated by hospital ships; such patients were defined as those "who may be expected to require considerable medical care enroute and much assistance in the event it becomes necessary to abandon ship." Other patients, it was said, "may be evacuated by regularly-scheduled returning personnel transports."

Overseas commanders are in general, responsible for:

"a.   Preliminary evacuation of patients from forward to rear areas within the command; their care until fit for further evacuation by water or air, and their concentration at sea or air ports from which they will be evacuated to the United States."

When the patients to be removed have been assembled, they are evacuated by the Army hospital ships operating on regular schedules. Priorities for return on hospital ships are set up, "without regard to the service status of the individual (Army, Navy, Coast Guard, Merchant Marine, United Nations, Civilian, Prisoner of War, Other), generally in accordance with the following:

(1) All female patients.

(2) Litter patients.

(3) Mental patients requiring security accommodations, especially major psychoses.

---

[71]   See AG 704.11 (3 June 1944) OB- S-E- SPMOT-M, Restricted. Attached to the letter are a number of inclosures composed chiefly of sample forms.

(4) Hospital ambulant patients requiring considerable medical care and assistance.

(5) Other hospital ambulant patients.

(6) Other mental patients.

(7) Troop class patients.

The Chief of Transportation, and under him the commanders of United States ports, "are responsible for patients evacuated by water from the time they pass from the control of the overseas commander until they are turned over to the commanding general of a service command." At the Charleston Port of Embarkation, where until recently all Army hospital ships have docked, the key figures in the evacuation process, under the Commanding General, are the Port Surgeon and the Superintendent of the Water Division, together with the Hospital Ship Commander.

At Washington, D. C. under the Chief of Transportation, Army Service Forces, the Water Division and the Movements Division occupy important roles in the evacuation of patients by water. After consultation with the Water Division (Aircraft and Troop Transport Branch) to determine the available Army hospital ships, the Movements Division (Convoy and Scheduling Branch) arranges the scheduling of such vessels.[72] Although the bulk of the work with respect to the conversion program has been completed, the Maintenance and Repair Branch and the Ship Conversion Unit, Water Division, still have (as of October 1944) two hospital ships to be completed. Much of the pioneering with regard to the designation and

---

[72] For details see Memorandum of 8 May 1944 by Brig. Gen. R. H. Wylie, Assistant Chief of Transportation and Director of Operations, transmitting revised operating procedure on scheduling of troop and hospital ship movements.

naming of the Army hospital ships has fallen to the Ship Operations Branch, Water Division. This Branch is also concerned with the administration and technical operation of these vessels, and in this connection it recently prepared a helpful U. S. Army Hospital Ship Guide.[73]

No account of current operations would be complete without mention of the vital part played by the Office of Surgeon General at every stage in the planning, conversion, and operation of the Army hospital ships. The Army hospital fleet as it exists today conforms so far as is practicable and feasible to the requirements of the Surgeon General. Together with the respective hospital ship commanders, the Port Surgeon at Charleston has a strategic position in the evacuation process. At Washington, D. C., the development of overall policy and procedure with respect to Army hospital ships, as well as the evacuation of patients by air and water, is at present the responsibility in particular of the Medical Regulating Unit headed by Lt. Colonel John C. Fitzpatrick as Medical Regulating Officer.

The Medical Regulating Unit

The Medical Regulating Unit is comparatively new. It was set up in May 1944 in order to meet anticipated requirements in connection with the evacuation of sick and wounded from overseas commands.[74] It operates under the Deputy Chief for Hospitals and Domestic Operations, Operations Service, Office of the Surgeon General, but its physical location is

---

[73] Published as TC Pamphlet No. 16, 1 August 1944.

[74] Circular No. 147, Army Service Forces, Section II, 19 May 1944, which is based upon Par. 9, WD Circular No. 140, 11 April 1944.

with the Movements Division, Office of the Chief of Transportation, "in order to permit closer coordination of effort and greater accessibility of information." It replaces the former Transportation Liaison Unit which had performed similar functions on a smaller scale. As of 30 June 1944 the new Unit consisted of seven officers and eleven civilians.

To meet the anticipated load of patients, the Medical Regulating Unit has made available hospital ship complements for all hospital ships in operation as well as for those still under conversion. Apart from the vital task of maintaining liaison with the Medical Regulating Offi- cer, Army Air Forces, and with the Movements Division, Water Division, and Traffic Control Division, Office of the Chief of Transportation, the Medical Regulating Unit is charged, in general, with assuring the "effi- cient utilization of available beds and minimum demands on transportation facilities."

Nature and Extent of the Current Evacuation Problem

The Medical Regulating Unit must cope with the entire problem of evacuating patients by water from all overseas theaters and commands. A few generalizations drawn from its annual report for the fiscal year 1944 illustrate the scope of the task at hand. During that period, because of the limitations of the turnaround and the relatively small number of vessels in operation, the Army hospital ships transported to the United States only about ten per cent of the total patient load evacuated by water. During the fiscal year 1944 the majority of the patients received in this way were debarked at San Francisco. For the same period the New York Port of Embarkation ranked second among the ports, while Hampton

Roads and Charleston proved close contenders for third and fourth places. A breakdown by the overseas commands from which patients were returned by water showed that for the same period the largest number came from North Africa. The next largest number came from the United Kingdom, although Australia and New Caledonia each furnished almost as large a contingent of the sick and wounded.

On 31 July 1944 the Army had 17 hospital ships in its service, with a total capacity of 9,500 beds. Seven other vessels were to be added at the end of 1944 to bring the total patient capacity to some 14,600 beds. The average turnaround time, however, greatly exceeds 30 days, so that far fewer than the present objective of 14,600 patients can be debarked per month in the United States. Returning troop transports must still be used for the great majority of the patients to be evacuated.

Certain hospital ships have been especially active in certain theaters, notably North Africa, where the Army hospital ship SEMINOLE carried 10,500 patients during the $5\frac{1}{2}$ months ended 10 July 1944. Hospital ships have also been used to a limited extent in support of amphibious operations as at Salerno. Hospital ships were not used in the Normandy invasion, and the initial evacuees from that operation were carried to England in LST's specially outfitted for this purpose.

During 1943 less than 5 per cent of roughly 70,000 evacuees to the United States arrived in hospital ships. During the first seven months of 1944 about 18 per cent of the total of 62,500 evacuees have been debarked from Army hospital ships. This figure compares with 16 per cent evacuated by air and 66 per cent by returning troopship.[75]

With intensive combat operations still in prospect both in Europe and in Asia, it may be assumed that the flow of casualties will continue and that the present fleet of Army hospital ships will be fully occupied for a long time to come. Upon the changing fortunes of war will depend the need of additional Army hospital ships in 1945.

---

[75] See Monthly Progress Report, Army Service Forces, Sec. 6, Analysis, 31 July 1944, pp. 83-84.

APPENDIX A

1. U. S. Army Hospital Ships, 1 November 1944

NAME	EX-NAME	STATUS	DATE ACQUIRED	PATIENT CAPACITY
ACADIA		SB	10-16-42	821
ALGONQUIN		SB	8-23-42	462
BLANCHE F. SIGMAN	Stanford White	AO	11-23-43	590
CHARLES A. STAFFORD	Siboney	BB	7-1- 42	706
CHATEAU THIERRY		AO	2-21-21	658
DOGWOOD	George Wash. Carver	AO	11-23-43	592
EMILY H.M. WEDER	Pres. Buchanan	BB	11-1- 43	738
ERNEST HINDS	Kent	AO	4-13-41	293
*ERNESTINE KORANDA	Dorothy Luckenbach	BB	7-19-44	732
JARRETT M. HUDDLESTON	Samuel F.B. Morse	AO	11-23-43	584
JOHN J. MEANY	Zebulon B. Vance	AO	11-23-43	582
JOHN L. CLEM	Irwin	AO	3-6- 41	270
LARKSPUR	Bridgeport	BB	9-11-43	586
*LOUIS A. MILNE	Lewis Luckenbach	BB	5-17-44	846
MARIGOLD	Pres. Fillmore	BB	10-8- 43	763
SEMINOLE		BB	5-22-43	456
SHAMROCK	Agwileon	BB	11-27-42	468
ST. MIHIEL		AO	7-22-43	506
ST. OLAF		AO	11-23-43	584
THISTLE	Munargo	AO	3-12-41	456
WISTERIA	William Osler	AO	11-23-43	601

AO - Army Owned
BB - Bareboat to Army by War Shipping Administration
SB - Sub-bareboat to Army by War Shipping Administration

*Under Conversion.

2. Navy Hospital Ships in the Service of the Army

NAME	HOME PORT	PATIENT CAPACITY
COMFORT	Los Angeles Port of Embarkation	705
HOPE	Los Angeles Port of Embarkation	705
MERCY	Los Angeles Port of Embarkation	705

3. Pending Conversions to Army Hospital Ships, December 1944

ATHOS II

COLOMBIE

PRESIDENT TYLER

REPUBLIC

SATURNIA

Note: The above-listed are tentative selections, subject to change.
Except for the REPUBLIC, the present names will not be retained.